Black Pearl

Pearls of Wisdom From Women of Color

Paulette Yancy Booth, Inspired Author

Book Cover by Veonne Anderson

"To My Daughters & Granddaughters "

And to All

"The Black Pearls"

Why This Book?

I believe that this book was placed in my spirit, or downloaded, if you will, by Father God, to remind women how unique and purposeful He designed us to be. I am under no delusion that this book is a brilliant first of its kind. But I do believe for such a time as this, we need perhaps a subtle reminder of His word, which as I have found to be so all inclusive for what our intended purpose was from the very beginning in the garden. My hopes are that we will be able to journey together with our earned and sometimes borrowed wisdom. Sharing our collective experiences, and in doing so, highlighting our individual life experiences takes us from our doubtful beginnings and boldly, but ever-so-humbly, makes us Powerful God-felt Sisterhood Influencers. So this book is a compilation of many experiences, journeys, and emotional victories. An overflow of wisdom for women of all ages, especially those that are seeking and hungry for truth, guidance, and answers that can be gleaned from sharing. So, for those who are prayerfully seeking and decide to journey with us and run towards a victorious life, join us. Let's partake together of this book I call "Pearls of Wisdom".

Why This Title?

"Black Pearl"

Pearls of Wisdom from Women of Color

The idea of the black pearl has always come with mystic and a soulful darkness, unlike the classic White Pearl, which has always been a symbol of prestige and elegance. It's a new day for the Black Pearl. My research has revealed this precious and sought-after gem is so befitting the theme of this book. Women of color are so diverse, so mysterious, and yes, sought-after. And like them, the black pearl has a very special legacy.

As with most things, there are some copycats that want the status, the intrigue, the value, the hue — and yes — the melanin of the black pearl. However, there is nothing quite like the real thing. It took some time for it to gain acceptance as an exotic pearl, but today, its mystery and intrigue have caused it to become famous the whole world over.

Here are some facts about this precious gem which explain exactly why it was chosen for the title of this book. The black pearl, also known as a Tahitian pearl, has been called the "Black Swan" of the jewelry world and is exceedingly rare. It is specifically produced by something called the "black-lipped oyster", or *Pinctada margaritifera*. This oyster is found in the tropical azure waters of French Polynesia.

The more curious reader may wonder *Where is that?* or *Who are the people there?* For those so interested in the deeper details of the location, you must do your own research. I do know enough to share with you that the people of French Polynesia are a beautiful race of people with a sun-kissed, bronze-and-honey colored skin complexion.

The black pearl itself, as it matures within the oyster, may take on many hues: shades of peacock green and pewter, blues, purples, and even blush reds. However, only in the Tahitian pearl will a naturally black color emerge. The black-lipped oyster usually only produces one pearl at a time, which takes several years to mature. This contributes directly to the black pearl's status as rare, unusual, and unique — and therefore why it enjoys such high demand. Today, gemologists claim that the "black pearl" is one of the most sought-after gems in the world.

In this book, I have the time to give only a brief overview of this precious gem. I implore you to do your own research and be amazed at the parallel between women of color and the black pearl.

I want to share a scripture with you that perhaps is most appropriate. Please feel free to read the entire chapter to receive even more insight as to what Father God was sharing with us:

"Again the Kingdom of heaven is like a merchant looking for fine pearls. When he found one of great value, he went away and sold everything he had and bought it." (Matthew

13: 45–46 (NIV)

The Cover Rose

The rose has many colors and meanings. Its colors, as well as their individual meanings, range from A to Z. As I have expressed previously to many of the supporters of my book, I can't take any credit for its design or content. Truly I know that the Lord was directing me as to His purpose and design. During the course of this journey I have seen the works of His creative hand. In the research that I did on the "White Rose", I was amazed that this Rose has much history and intentional sentiment that follows it. Depending on the occasion and culture, the white rose can relay a myriad of heartfelt emotions: purity, marriage, loyalty, youthfulness, innocence, new beginnings, and young love — Love being one of its most emphasized special qualities.

The white rose is steeped in ancient Greek mythology deeply rooted in Love (which is an entire tale of its own, very romantic). In my search, I found that the white rose is symbolic in traditional Christianity, representing purity and joy. It is also associated with the individual who is graduating or moving away, given as an expression of support, well wishes, and the very best for the journey ahead — symbolizing the restoring of balance in life, new beginnings in life, and hoping that the recipient(s) will experience good health and a prosperous future. The white rose and its many meanings are a timeless beauty.

The cover "White Rose" is transverse and the black pearl descends from it. I believe this represents the uniqueness of the black pearl. It has been nestled in all the beauty, love, purity, kindness, concern, and generosity associated with the white rose and symbolizes the belief in God, ready to go forth and share, giving all it has to give to those who seek all its attributes — with *Love* as the core.

"I am the Rose of Sharon, and the lily of the valleys. As the lily among thorns, so is my love among my daughters." (Song of Solomon 2: 1–2)

There is No Cost

I believe the new buzz word in the writing world is *transparency*. I intend to give my readers just that.

With what is happening in our world today, things appear to be — if I may borrow a phrase — "straight crazy". Young people have so much to consider, to decide, to emulate, and to ponder — the list goes on and on. The internet, social media, and cell phones are major contributors to the massive changes in the lives of our youth. But what is going on exactly in our world today? I can't really ask that question without thinking of Marvin Gaye's classic "What's Going On".

God said, in His word, that if we asked Him for wisdom, He would willingly give it to us (see James 1: 5). So what is the definition of *wisdom*? According to Oxford Languages, it is "the quality of having experience, knowledge, and good judgment; the quality of being wise."

I want to be sure that we understand all of this definition, though. Let's take a closer look at the words *knowledge, good,* and *judgment.* According to Oxford, the definition of knowledge is "facts, information, and skills acquired by a person through experience or education; the theoretical or practical understanding of a subject."

Now what about the definition of judgment? "The ability to make considered decisions or come to a sensible conclusion" (also from the Oxford dictionary).

Fortunately, the word "good" is quite self-explanatory.

All of these descriptions and explanations of the word *wisdom* are at least secularly correct. However, more to the point, the word of God tells us that we who believe can freely ask God for wisdom, and He will willingly give it to us. According to God, there are no prerequisites to receiving wisdom other than asking and believing. I included the definition of *wisdom* because I thought that a better understanding and clarification of the word could begin to help us see how we need doses of it in our lives daily. Stay with me, because we're going to continue to bring more clarity to the subject which will prove how valuable and priceless this wisdom really is.

"The Lord giveth Wisdom: out of His mouth cometh Knowledge and understanding." (Proverbs 2: 6)

What Exactly Does the Bible Say about Wisdom?

Here is a glance into God's word regarding the topic of wisdom. Read and be blessed:

Proverbs 1: 7 (NLT)

"The fear of God is the beginning of Wisdom..."

Proverbs 2: 6 (NLT)

"Tune your ears to wisdom, and concentrate on understanding..."

Proverbs 13: 10 (NLT)

"Pride leads to arguments; those who take advice are wise."

Jeremiah 9: 23–24

"Thus saith the Lord, Let not the wise man glory in his Wisdom... But let him that glorieth glory in this, that he Understandeth and knoweth me..."

Hosea 14: 9

"Let those who are wise understand these things. Let those who are discerning listen carefully..."

Matthew 7: 24

"Anyone who listens to my teaching and obeys me is wise..."

James 1:5

"If any man lack wisdom, let him ask God, that He giveth to all men liberally...

I invite you to delve into these scriptures so that you will know the power of God's word concerning Wisdom. Be equipped for the journey.

When We Share

One day during the publishing process, my book coordinator and I were discussing the dynamics of this book. I was so filled with joy, with excitement and purpose. As she listened, she kept telling me to simply "preach". You know, that's what we often say when a message is on point or extremely relatable. This, for me, was confirmation as to why I believe this book and its content are from God for such a time as this.

I shared with her that in this fast-paced world we're living in, sometimes I'll hear a young lady say, "Oh, that's *old school*," and the connotation behind the statement is that "That doesn't apply" or "That's no longer relevant." When I hear this, it really gets me to thinking: when did *God's word* stop being relevant? When did it change? I didn't get that update in my Bible.

The response I shared with one such young lady after she made that comment is that many of us living today are thriving exactly because of *old school*. The wisdom that was imparted to us and then (perhaps oftentimes reluctantly) taken actually brought about great successes and even saved our lives, helped us raise our children correctly, gave us the ability to challenge ourselves to do better and to think higher. I told her that oftentimes when our elders are trying to share their wisdom with us, it is not because they are so very educated or have master's or doctorate degrees, but because their life's journey has taught them, engaged them, caused them to reflect upon and rethink that particular part of their journey. In other words, they have "been there; done that" and have personally seen the outcome or the consequences of these situations. I also shared with her how fortunate we are to cross paths with women who are *willing* to share with us, pray with us, encourage us, and point us to the path that leads to success and all the good things that Father God wants his sons and daughters to partake of.

One of the things I often share with my daughters when we're deep in discussion, with views flying everywhere and yet wisdom not yet being caught, is this: "If my word is not what you want to hear, go find another mature person that you respect and admire and ask *them* about the issue instead — and then listen to what they share."

In the history of the Bible, Ruth chose to stay with her mother-in-law Naomi after all of her tragedy and misfortune. She heard her mother-in-law's sage advice and heeded it, and as a consequence, Ruth was rewarded with a loving, God-fearing husband — and much more. The fruit of Ruth and Boaz's union ended up becoming the lineage of Jesus Christ. I recommend reading Ruth chapter 3, verses 1 through 13. Actually, I recommend reading the entire book of Ruth. Be amazed at how wisdom was imparted and caught. I love it.

A Closer Look at Biblical Influencers

Heroines of Their Day

I have a personal love for Proverbs chapter 31. It describes what I like to call a "Bad Mama Jama" — the first Super Woman, if you will. This woman was able to do in one day what most people would need a full staff to accomplish. Her description is given by King Lemuel's mother, who hopes to prepare him by offering "Pearls of Wisdom" for selecting a wife.

She begins by stating that "she" (this ideal woman) is a virtuous woman and a capable wife. What does the word *virtuous* mean? Well, according to Oxford Languages, there are *forty-seven other adjectives* which can describe the state of being virtuous. I, however, will share only the first and the last adjectives used. The first one is "righteous", and the last one is "squeaky clean".

The king's mother then speaks of the value of a good woman, appraising her as worth more than rubies. She continues her description of the ideal wife, and she is very precise as to the type of mate her son should seek.

I challenge you to read this entire chapter, as many times as necessary, to understand the value that such a wife has according to King Lemuel's mother. But, for ease of reading, I will attempt to paraphrase the description of this phenomenal woman / wife below:

She is trustworthy; she is enriching; she will have her husband's back all the days of their lives; she is a seamstress; she brings in exotic foods for her family to feast on; she rises before dawn to prepare breakfast for her family and house staff; she prepares the duties of the day for the staff, she purchases land, and uses the land to plant a vineyard; she is strong and full of energy; she is a hard worker; she is thrifty; she stays up late preparing; she is a maker of cloth; she reaches out to the poor and welcomes in the needy; she has prepared garments to keep her entire household warm in cold weather; she has made a quilt for each bed; her garments are that of royalty; her husband is well-known in the community and he has status; her seamstress skills allow her to sell her items to vendors in the market; her character is one of strength and dignity; she beams with confidence in her future; she speaks with wisdom, and kindness is her mode of instruction; she watches and is vigilant for that which pertains to her household; she stays prepared; her family adores her and blesses her; her husband gives her praise; she surpasses all expectations. Charm is deceptive and beauty does not last, but a woman who fears the Lord will be greatly praised. She shall be rewarded for all that she has done. Her deeds will openly declare her praise.

Please take the time to read this chapter in full. For me, it is a constant reminder that there is so much to strive for and endless possibilities for self growth for both married and single women. Father God has given us a wonderful role model to give us the ability to keep growing, keep seeking, keep improving, keep accomplishing, keep learning, and keep challenging ourselves to become all that we were intended to be.

Proverbs 31
(read entire chapter)
Were you encouraged to set goals for yourself?

_____

_____

_____

_____

_____

_____

_____

_____

_____

_____

_____

Did you see some of your own attributes in her?

What did you find noteworthy about her?

Could this biblical wife be a contemporary woman?

List her pearls of wisdom that were described.

I think it is time to revisit another Biblical woman whom we can look to and learn from. This woman, despite and throughout tragic loss and displacement, was always obedient and faithful. She chose to listen to the Pearls of Wisdom which changed her entire life and many generations of the future. The woman of whom I speak was Ruth.

I ask myself, could I have done what she did? After losing her husband, father-in-law, and brother-in-law, Ruth chose to stay with her mother-in-law despite facing no legal obligation to do so. Her mother-in-law actually bade her return to her family, but Ruth chose to stay. They both struggled, as there was practically no income to take care of their day-to-day needs — but they struggled together. Now Naomi, the mother-in-law, could easily see the faithfulness in Ruth, and she knew that there was some good that could come out of such dire circumstances. She shared, once again, her Pearls of Wisdom with her daughter-in-law, which led Ruth to marry a wealthy man. Their marriage would begin the lineage of Jesus Christ. Once again, if you haven't read this Bible story, I exhort you to do so. It is absolutely amazing to me how sharing Pearls of Wisdom can be so life-changing.

Ruth
(read entire chapter)

What qualities in Ruth did you see as a daughter in-law?

_____

_____

_____

_____

_____

_____

_____

_____

_____

_____

List Naomi's (mother-inlaw)"Pearls of Wisdom"
that were shared with Ruth.

How did Ruth listening to her Mother-in-laws
"Pearls of Wisdom" change her life?

_____

_____

_____

_____

_____

_____

_____

_____

_____

_____

_____

How did Ruth's obedience affect generations to come?

_____

_____

_____

_____

_____

_____

_____

_____

_____

_____

_____

_____

_____

_____

Another Biblical woman whom I admire and marvel at for her "Pearls of Wisdom" ended up saving her entire family after her husband insulted the king of Israel by not showing hospitality to his troops while they were journeying. That king was King David, and the woman was called Abigail. After the king's request for accommodation was rejected by Abigail's husband, King David's response was to order the death of Abigail's husband — along with everyone else in his household.

At that, a servant who overheard the king's command raced to the home of Abigail and shared the fate that would shortly fall on their entire house. Abigail immediately gave the servant instructions to swiftly gather up all of the requested food and supplies for King David and his men and deliver them, while Abigail herself lagged behind. She, clearly heeding her "Pearls of Wisdom", employed a strategy to let the offering of food and supplies precede her arrival, which would surely soften the king's demeanor towards her household.

When Abigail finally arrived following her household's offering, she met King David with a humble spirit and with words of praise and prophecy. King David then looked upon Abigail as a wise woman, a woman of great value. Do you see any shared characteristics between Abigail and the "ideal wife" of Proverbs chapter 31? Amazing how wisdom appears to be key. By following wisdom, Abigail saved her household from the wrath of King David and certain death. In turn, he remembered Abigail for being a good woman and wife, and for her wisdom. After Abigail saved the day and went home to share her victory with her husband, he became so despondent over how he had responded to the king that he died a few days later. Shortly thereafter, King David heard of the death of Abigail's husband and sent for her to become his wife instead.

Abigail
(read 1 Samuel 25th chapter)

What did Abigail's husband do that angered King David?

_____

_____

_____

_____

_____

_____

_____

_____

By using wisdom how did she change the fate of her Household?

_____

_____

_____

_____

_____

_____

_____

_____

_____

_____

_____

_____

What were the specific acts that were
orchestrated by Abigail?

How was Abigail rewarded by her
"Pearls of Wisdom"?

These three women of the Bible are truly role models for all generations of women. They were 'influencers' long before social media coined the phrase. Their individual journeys displayed strength, courage, obedience, and wisdom — but most of all, a relationship with God.

The Letters

The Woman in the Mirror

The Sisterhood of Christian Women

Expression of Life Through Faith, a Haiku Poem

Looking Back but Moving Forward in Him

The Help Meet

Oh, What Joy

Message from the Heart

Dear Daughter

A Praying Mama

Don't Worry... It Won't Change a Thing (Prayer • Faith • Obedience)

Attitude

I am Persuaded, for HE is Good

I'm Thankful for My Mom's Wisdom

The Woman in the Mirror

Women and mirrors go together like bread and butter. Women use mirrors to see themselves throughout the day to make sure they are ready for the world to see. We often look at that woman in the mirror as she looks back at us and, on one hand, we are satisfied with the hair, the makeup, and the outfit — but then we get disgusted at the mole on her cheek, or the birthmark on her shoulder, or the slightly crooked smile that makes her prefer to shy away from pictures. Then we begin to go down this rabbit hole of thought: *Maybe I'm not pretty enough; If only I were taller; If only I didn't have this gap in my teeth; If only God hadn't made me this way.* It's like a roller coaster ride. All because you simply looked in the mirror!

When God said He knitted you in the womb and that you were fearfully and wonderfully made, He really *meant* that! (see Psalms 139: 13–14). When He said that He made you in

His own image, that means that *He made no mistakes.* (see Genesis 1: 27) God sees beyond what is reflected at you in the mirror — and what He sees is good!

There are things that make you uniquely *you*, and that is what He took time to do while you were being developed in your mother's womb. God needs your unique talents, personality, and experiences to encourage other women like you.

Whenever we don't see what God sees, we are falling into the enemy's trap. Anytime that the devil has an opportunity to take our attention away from our God-given purpose and calling, he jumps on it. Casting doubt on the beauty of who you are and what God created you to be is one of his preferred tricks. Do *not* let him win!

God made you for a specific purpose, and when He sees you, He sees His unique creation, whose beauty is beyond measure. He sees the beauty in the lives that will be touched because of you. He sees the beauty of who will see Him because of you.

The next time you look in the mirror and you start looking for things to not like, ask God to instead help you to see who He sees. You will be amazed at the reflection when you look at yourself from His perspective!

Rhonda L. Williams

CEDA Energy Services, Associate Director

The Sisterhood of Christian Women

I'm a single mother and now a grandmother of three. I remember always being a helper — even staying behind to help my mom with housework until she had to shoo me out of the house like a fly to go play outside. As a single mom, I've raised two children and helped my youngest daughter, who is also a single mom, to raise her three children. My eldest daughter suffered a traumatic brain injury when she was hit by a car in her youth. I'm still helping my 85-year-old mom — even while holding down a full-time job myself and serving in various church ministries. So, life has been a little challenging for me, and through it all, I've learned to trust God to supply my needs — and sometimes He uses the sisterhood of Christian women!

I began to fully experience the sisterhood of Christian women when I became a member of my local church. It brings me to tears whenever I remember the love and care shown to me by my sisters in Christ. For example: on one

Sunday morning, I was so overwhelmed by my life's challenges and a recent family squabble that by the time I reached church for our Sunday morning Service, I was so overcome with sadness and despair that I could not stay in my seat. I turned and fled back through the outer doors which I had passed through only moments earlier. I will never be able to forget how, as I stood alone and cried there on the steps of the church, a group of women from church came to me, surrounded me, and began to pray over me as I sobbed. They prayed earnestly and fervently for me while drying my tears. After a while with them, I felt the peace of God wash over me, and I returned to the Service feeling so much lighter than when I had arrived that morning.

Many times I have relied on the kindness and love of the sisterhood of Christian women to get me through the hard challenges of life. They have prayed with me and shared their successes and experiences (both good and bad) to encourage me and strengthen me in my own Christian walk. They have made themselves available to assist me with obstacles which were seemingly small, but to me were huge mountains. The sisterhood of Christian women touches me deeply, helping me and inspiring me to continue to run this Christian race with gusto and love.

"As iron sharpens iron, so one person sharpens another." (Proverbs 27: 17 NIV)

Shelia Coleman,

Altar Worker Co-Lead

Website Administrator & Graphic Designer

Victory In Christ Kingdom Church

Chicago, IL

"Expression of Life Through Faith", A Haiku Poem

Anxiously waiting

Becoming a new person

Carefully thinking

Danger is about

Expecting divine orders

Fearlessly faithful

Grateful assistance

Hope is believable now

Judging my steps to

Keep negativity back

Loving direction

Manipulative

Naysayers need not come near

Open my eyes now

Purification

Quantifying messages

Respectful always

Self-care agenda

Taking time to pray to YAH

Ms. Dolley T. James, M.S., M.Ed.

Licensed Educator / School Counselor

(*Haiku* is a form of poetry originating in Japan that focuses on a brief moment in time and a sense of sudden illumination or enlightenment for the reader.)

(*YAH — the Hebrew name for God, hewbrew4christians.com)

Looking Back but Moving Forward in Him

What I've learned most about being married and divorced twice is that God has given me the strength needed to grow and learn on this journey called life.

1. What do you value most in any relationship?

2. Name 3 things you'd like to have in common with your partner.

3. What do you believe is your best quality?

4. What aspect do you need personal growth in?

Life is about having faith and learning to trust someone other than yourself to get you to where you aspire to be. *"For I know the plans I have for you", says the Lord. "They are plans for good and not disaster, to give you a future and a hope".* Jeremiah 29: 11

As I continue to grow, I learn something new every day. I continually visualize the future I want for myself and my family. Patience is what I've learned to work on the most. I've also witnessed my growth and how I listen much more closely to that soft voice in my ear. I know that it is God's voice whispering what I need to hear at the exact moment that I need it. Did you know — patience is evidence of the Holy Spirit working in our lives.

"But the fruit of the Spirit is love, joy, peace, long suffering, gentleness, faith, meekness, temperance: against such there is no law." (Galatians 5: 22)

If there's one thing that 50-year-old Angela would have said to 21-year-old Angela, it would have been to enjoy life and to partner with God for the ride of your life. Prepare while in your youth to secure yourself as you reach your golden years. There are several parables and scriptures in the word that let us know that God wants us to be wise with our finances, but most importantly, to seek wisdom from God always as we journey.

"Charge them that are rich in this world, that they be not high minded, nor trust in uncertain riches, but in the living God, who giveth us richly all things to enjoy: that they do good, that be rich in good works, ready to distribute, willing to communicate; Laying up in store for themselves a good foundation against the time to come, that they may lay hold on eternal life." (1 Timothy 6: 17–19)

God's word is absolutely amazing.

Signed,

Angel Lynn Yancy

Angela Lynn Beaton

Angela Yancy Alexander

Angela

Business Woman and Entrepreneur

World Traveler

The Help Meet

...that divine assignment that God has given to every female. We are first introduced to this important assignment in Genesis chapter 2, verse 20. Adam was given authority by God to give names to all of the animals in Eden. Then it reads, *But for Adam, there was not found a "helper" or a help "fit" for him.*

This was the primary reason that God created the female. Whether you are married or single, this God-given calling will always arise in you and me, whatever the relationship is to the men in our lives.

Stop now and think about the men in your life — your husband, your father, your brother, your grandson, your nephew, your boss, your friend, and on and on. With each name that comes to your mind, I bet you can remember, at least once, the GREAT help to them that you were and are.

So, my dear women, my dear ladies, my beautiful sisters everywhere — know that you are a valuable female created by God! You are a valuable asset for those whose lives God has assigned to you. (Remember, I wrote that God assigned them to you!) Know that you have been given a special calling that was put into your DNA. You had no choice.

But you *do* have a choice in how you use this special gift from God. It must be used to glorify God in the lives of those you have been called by GOD to come alongside and serve. Know that serving others begins with serving God.

Never look down on yourselves. Never settle for anyone who devalues you. Never settle for any kind of abuse, whether physical, sexual, financial, or emotional. As helpers fit for the "him"s in your life, know that God has not called you to walk behind nor to walk in front of. You are called to walk *beside*.

Guess what? Effectiveness in being that fit and effective helper *begins* with your relationship with God through Jesus Christ.

Do you have that relationship?

Dr. Theresa Bowen

Minister

Oh, What Joy

In this journey called life, I have learned that we all have a purpose in making a difference in the lives of others. We are the light of the world.

"Ye are the light of the world. A city that is set on a hill cannot be hidden." (Matthew 5: 14)

We were created in the image of God and belong to Him; every breath I take is only because of Him. Knowing this, He must be my guide.

"And be not conformed to this world: but be ye transformed by the renewing of your mind, that ye may prove what is that good, and acceptable, and perfect, will of God." (Romans 12: 2)

God's deliverance is beyond our grasp, His thoughts regarding grace by far exceeds anything man could ever imagine. With this in mind, we must continue to trust in His Word, even with limited knowledge. I thank and praise God for the seed that is planted within me and watered by Him. For it is He alone that will give me the natural and spiritual nourishment that I need now and forever.

"Then shall we know, if we follow on to know the LORD: his going forth is prepared as the morning; and he shall come unto us as the rain, as the latter and former rain unto the earth." (Hosea 6: 3)

I know for myself that God is always faithful and cleanses us.

"If we confess our sins to him, he is faithful and just to forgive us our sins and to cleanse us from all unrighteousness." (1 John 1:9)

No matter the circumstance, I must continually hold to God's truth as my standard of living.

"Preach the word; be instant in season, out of season; reprove, rebuke, exhort with all long suffering and doctrine." (2 Timothy 4: 2)

So, in this journey called life, let us be an encouragement to others as our Lord and Savior, Jesus Christ.

"Wherefore comfort yourselves together, and edify one another, even as also ye do." (1 Thessalonians 5: 11)

There is a uniqueness in us all. Whatever spiritual gift is given by God, know that it is empowered by the Holy Spirit. Therefore, use your spiritual gift for God's glory.

"But the Comforter, which is the Holy Ghost, whom the Father will send in my name, he shall teach you all things, and bring all things to your remembrance, whatsoever I have said unto you." (John 14: 26)

I can never fully love as Jesus Christ — however, using Him as my guide, I can be an example of His love.

Humbly Submitted,

Mira Davis

Rush University Medical Center — Chicago, IL

Administrator

Message from the Heart

Jesus told us in Matthew 7: 7 that everyone who asks shall receive. Make sure you're asking the Lord for your highest good in every situation. Always feel blessed and be careful what you think, because like King Solomon said in Psalms 4: 23, your thoughts run your life. Always enjoy this very moment in your life and do not think about your past — it could mess up this moment and more in the future to come. Wake up every morning counting your blessings and thanking God for all that you have. When you lay your head on your pillow, go over your day feeling grateful and mapping out the Great Day you will have the next day. Become wise by walking with the wise; hang out with fools and watch your life fall to pieces (see Proverbs 13: 20).

Make sure you marry someone who has similar values to yours. They say 90% of your life, whether joyful or miserable, depends on who you marry — and once you *do* marry, you have to commit to each other that divorce is not an option, but rather telling the truth in love will make all the difference. Put God first in all your relationships, because talking to the Lord for help when you need it is key. Forgive yourself, and others, because we all fall short of the glory of God. Lastly, let your parents (or whoever was involved in your upbringing) off the hook and forgive them, because the first step towards your healing and ultimate happiness is self-acceptance, and knowing that you're an adult equips you to truly start your journey.

Gloria Roberson

Mother of 4 courageous adults and wife to Lee Roberson for 31 years

Dear Daughter

I hope you don't mind me addressing you as, daughter. I'm older now and I take great pleasure in encouraging young women as I would my own daughters. I have three beautiful daughters. I have had the joy of birthing into the world. Today, they are young married women with children of their own, and yet they still come to me for advice. I also have many young and older women I call my spiritual daughters, in whose lives I have had the privilege of speaking. And now, I also have the pleasure of imparting words of wisdom to you! So again, I hope you don't mind if I refer to you as ,daughter!

Daughter, the thing I want to say to you is very important to your success in life, so please listen carefully! You have been given the gift of life; Praise the Lord! The Word of God tells us this: *"And the Lord God formed man of the dust of the ground, and breathed into his nostrils the breath of life..."* (Genesis 2: 7). *"Then the rib which the Lord God had taken from man He made into a woman, and He brought her to the man."* (Gen. 2: 22)

David said, *"I will praise you, for I am fearfully and wonderfully made; marvelous are Your works, and that my soul knows very well."* (Psalm 139: 14)

Jesus said, *"I have come that you may have life and that more abundantly."* (John 10: 10)

However, you have the challenge of living out your life to please God in a fallen world, with great temptations, distractions, fleshly desires, and a dark adversary! Because of all of this, you need some help to successfully reach your God-given destiny in life. Many women have tried to live life on their own only to wind up disappointed, discouraged, and disillusioned. The Good News is that *Jesus died* to send us the helper we need. The Holy Spirit is the person sent by God to walk with you through this life. Jesus told His disciples that it was to their advantage that He go away so that He could send them the Helper to get them successfully through life.

Jesus said, *"For if I do not go away, the Helper will not come to you; but if I depart, I will send Him to you."* (John 16: 7)

The Holy Spirit is in the world to help the Believer in Jesus get through life successfully. I thank God for His help! I have found that there is no help like the help of the Holy Spirit! And daughter, He will help you, too! All you have to do is ask for His help!

Pastor Caren Susberry

Victory in Christ Kingdom Church

Chicago, IL

A Praying Mama

Since I can remember, prayer has been at the very core of my being. I remember at a very young age my mother going through our family home praying and singing old hymns. As my life progressed, I perhaps didn't fully understand that God was right there with me. Sometimes in my world, it felt like there was a constant turbulent wind all around me. But He truly was right there.

"I will never leave you nor forsake you." (Hebrews 13: 5)

There isn't enough time or paper to fully share God's goodness, but I am convinced that prayer has kept me and my family. My children, now fully grown, have seen me on my knees crying out in prayer. My husband has seen how prayer has worked on our behalf with miracles that could have only come from a Heavenly Father.

"Rejoice always, praying without ceasing, in everything give thanks for this the will of God in Christ Jesus for you." (1 Thessalonians 5: 16–18)

I would like to encourage the reader of this letter to know that there is Power in sincere Prayer to God. I have learned that no matter what things look like, our God is ready to renew, restore, refresh, rectify, and rebuild anything for those who turn to Him. He Loves us.

I am a grandmother. I'm so grateful that all my children know and have experienced the Power of Prayer and will readily pray and even ask me to pray for them. Now I have a new grandbaby who will hear his Nana pray. Prayer has become a direct line to God and a way of life for me.

May you also enter this direct line with Him so you, your children, and your entire family, too, may experience His Love.

Caroline Sahara-Wells

Healthy Start

Program Director

Don't Worry... It Won't Change a Thing!

Prayer • Faith • Obedience

Prayer: *"I call on you, my God, for you will answer me; turn your ear to me and hear my prayer."* (Psalm 17: 6)

Faith: *"Now then stand still and see this great thing the Lord is about to do before your Eyes."* (1 Samuel 12: 6)

Obedience: *"And the Lord said, I will do the very thing you have asked, because I am pleased with you and I know you by name."* (Exodus 33: 17)

Prayer, Faith and Obedience will change everything in your Life. You will be blessed by the Grace of God with vision, wisdom, and testimony of what the Lord can do and has done in your life.

It is said, "If you worry, don't pray" — but if you want change in your life, have faith in your prayers (requests), pray for what you want (request), and be obedient to the answer you receive from the Lord for your Blessings!

Nyla D. Rease

Field Interviewer

Institute for Social Research, University of Michigan

Attitude

"Do all things without grumbling or complaining, that you may be blameless and innocent, children of God without blemish in the midst of a crooked and twisted generation, among whom you shine as lights in the world." (Philippians 2: 14–15)

I have complained about the smallest things in my life and found myself feeling so ashamed. After such complaining, I would often say to myself, "I *know* I did not just say that out loud!"

My grumbling was always because I took my eyes off of Jesus and let negative thoughts cloud my mind, just as Peter did when he stepped out of the boat and began to sink in the water, he similarly took his eyes off of Jesus (see Matthew 14: 29–31). In order to do what Jesus does, I have to "Do" what (Philippians 4: 9) says to "Do". I want to learn His values, so the complaining will come to a halt. I study to receive His attitude, so that His Spirit shines through me. I want to hear that still small voice whisper in my ear: *"Well done."* I want to see what He has seen in me.

So that means that I have to "Do". I have to study and learn the will of God for my life and be content with such things as I have in the midst of a crooked and twisted generation. I must decree, through my actions — through what I "Do" — that I have the mind and attitude of Christ Jesus and that I shine as a light in the world.

Darlene McGee

Retired Home Daycare Owner

I am Persuaded, for HE is Good

God's Grace and Mercy kept me when I did not really know Him. He makes me better and shows me how to love others. One of the major things God has taught me is that words have *power*. We must use our words carefully and lovingly.

Proverbs 31: 26 (KJV) says, "*She opens her mouth with wisdom, and the teaching of kindness is on her tongue.*"

God gets the Glory when we share truth, love, and wisdom. Positive words that are reinforced by positive actions can be life-changing for us, personally, and for all those to whom we are attached. Choose to uplift, not to tear down. The elders would always say "If you don't have anything good to say, don't say anything."

I would like to change that. *Reframe* what you would say and say it with love and kindness. Proper communication is key in all relationships. Don't just suppress how you feel and hold back what you need to say; instead, choose to say it with wisdom and kindness.

If the situation is not positive and you don't have the words, *pause* and say nothing for a period of time. Join the *Shut Up* Ministry. Be still and *pray*. Give it to God and wait for His direction. God is in control of all things. Do not carry any unnecessary burdens. Trust God with all things and live a life of Grace. Show others the same Grace that you would want to receive.

Love covers all in every relationship.

Kecia Ellis Bobbitt

Prayer Warrior, Intercessor, Encourager, Daughter, Sister, Wife, Mom, Mentor, Financial Services Professional

I'm Thankful for My Mom's Wisdom

One day I woke up and realized that I was sounding just like my mom. Using the very same words in my marriage and with my children, and even using her as a reference for life issues.

Let me share a little about my mom. She dropped out of high school to marry my dad. She still knew the importance of a high school diploma, so she enrolled herself into night school, through which she received her diploma. I can testify by virtue of having grown up in her house that she sought wisdom very early in her life.

Now, let me be perfectly honest, at that time in my early years, I was unaware of the true meaning of wisdom. My mom's childhood had been very turbulent, however, I know that God's hand of protection held her. It enabled her at an early age to make wise decisions and navigate her life using her belief and trust in God. Even as a young girl and as she became a young woman, she was surrounded by mature women who were very impactful during her early years. I remember hearing her tell various stories in which their wisdom was specifically given to her.

One account I remember her sharing involved an older neighbor who would sit on her front porch on the route that my mom would take to school every day. Apparently this wise woman kept a watchful eye on her community, which included my mom. On one particular day, my mom was accompanied home by a young boy who wanted to carry her books and walk her to her house. The old woman sitting on her front porch kindly (and shamelessly) shouted out to my mom, "Look, gal, I don't want to see you with that boy any more — he's got two girls pregnant now, and you'll be next." When my mother heard this, she realized that she did not want to be his next victim. She listened to wise counsel, and forthright ended that acquaintance.

Another instance in which wisdom directed my mom in the right direction took place after she had an upset with my dad. After this particular fight, she was determined that she would leave him, even though the marriage was quite new and already my two oldest brothers were born. I was quite amused at this story when I first heard it, but now, I think I truly understand her thought process. She packed up her belongings along with my brothers and all of her household things — the kitchen curtains, too. Everything fit into only one suitcase.

It was at this point that a close and older friend of hers intervened. She was very direct, expressing to my mom that leaving my dad would not be beneficial, due to her circumstances at the time. She had nowhere to go with two young children, no money, and not enough experience to know that marriage *does* take time and work. Oh, and lots of prayer. It's obvious that she listened, because I myself am now here. Thank God.

What I realize from these stories is that my mom made good decisions by relying on much prayer and wisdom imparted from her elders. She was able to navigate her life by adhering to wise counsel.

It was my mother's father and his wisdom that inspired my parents to relocate from the South to the North. Here, my family would begin to prosper. You see, I never experienced what my family's earlier plight was. I grew up living in what my mom would call the "New World". It was listening to wisdom and her trust and belief in God that transformed my family's life.

"Who is wise and he shall understand these things? Prudent, and he shall know them? For the ways of the Lord are right, and the just shall walk in them..." (Hosea 14: 9)

Paying Homage

I didn't want to end this time with you, dear reader, without sharing that throughout my personal journey, I have been beyond honored by some absolutely remarkable "Pearls" of women. These women have all in some way influenced me, although many may never know their actual impact. I believe that each one of us has had some "Pearl" to inspire us, encourage us, challenge us, set us straight, catch us, and most of all, help us to be better. As women, we are charged to help one another. So let's do just that.

Here, I acknowledge some personally-known and some well-known women, some still present and some who have passed on. Regardless of their status, their contributions are and have been a powerful force for women everywhere.

Courtne Davis*   Lillian Hinkle*

Rose Porter*   Ruby Jones*

Harriett Tubman   Maya Angelou

Ella Moman*   Clorissa Keyes*

Anna Laura Yancy*   Madam C.J. Walker

Katherine Harris*   Dr. Shirley Ann Jackson

Viola Andrews*   Ida B. Wells

Margaret McCrimmon*   Flora Stewart

Yolanda Beatty*   Debra Edwards*

Janice Pamon*   Carol Hemphill*

Oprah Winfrey   Thelma Taylor*

Geraldine Yancy*   Whoopi Goldberg

June Andrews*   Valerie Anderson*

Ada Copeland King   Caroline S. Wells*

Willa Guess*   Lillian Ingram*

Pastor Caren Susberry*   Sheila Dixon*

Sarah Rector   Polly Jackson*

(an asterisk * denotes one of the personal influencers in my life)

Snippets of Wisdom from Women of Color

"Let us not speak about one another with a negative intent, because the ability to restrain our tongue is a virtue."

—Margaret McCrimmon (Psalms 35: 28)

"Live Life with a light touch."

—Thelma Taylor

"Wisdom is having the ability to know what to do, how to do it, when it is needed to be done."

—Patricia A. Whitehead

"Be ever so mindful of what you say."

—Mary Wells (Proverbs 18: 21)

"Love God first before anything. Keep your mind on Him."

—Gloria Billings (Mark 12: 30)

"You must reach them where they are to take them where you want to go."

—Gail Howard Johnson

"Craziness takes place when we engage in repetitive behavior with an expectancy of change."

—Paulette Yancy Booth

"The Father has entrusted you with love and wisdom to make sound decisions about life in Him."

—Patricia A. Whitehead

"Be proactive instead of reactive."

—Paulette Yancy Booth

"There's a million unseen hands supporting your journey."

—Tiara Scott

My Dear Reader,

My prayer for you after taking this journey with us is that your spirit may have been lifted and transformed because you have captured Wisdom through God's inspired women. I hope that one, or two, or perhaps each letter you read may have left its mark on you in some remarkable way. Whatever the case may be, I thank you for your steadfastness in completing this book.

I also wish to extend a very special *Thank You* to all of the women who journeyed with me through these inspirational letters, and to all of my friends and family who cheered this project on. I am encouraged, and you should be as well. Let us look around, prayerfully, within our spheres of influence and ask Father God to lead and guide us to continue to help, encourage, and testify to His Goodness.

My final recommendation to you would be to open your Bible to the Epistle to Titus, chapter 2. I might suggest a specific focus on verses 3 and 4, regarding how the older women must teach the younger women, but please do not stop there. Read the entire chapter and be blessed.

Thank you,

Paulette

So Inspired

About Paulette

Once you meet Paulette, and have the opportunity to really know her over time, you are sure to discover a beautifully complicated person with an abundance of positive affirmations. She is loving, giving, knowledge-seeking, fun-loving, and perhaps most importantly, a devout and faithful follower of Jesus Christ, as revealed in this book.

Paulette loves unconditionally. Once she knows you and accepts you as a true friend, you will experience her caring and loving nature, and you will delight in the experience.

She gives and shares with little effort. What she has can easily become yours once a friendship is established. Although life can be complicated with its many challenges, Paulette always manages to see the "lighter" sides. Laughter for her frequently becomes the cure-all for the obstacles which life presents to her.

Finally, and most importantly, she holds firmly and with true conviction to her unwavering belief in Jesus Christ which has sustained and continues to sustain her as she journeys through life.

-    Ralph Yancy, Educator

www.ingramcontent.com/pod-product-compliance
Lightning Source LLC
Chambersburg PA
CBHW071944100426
42737CB00046BA/2481